CONTENTS

ZOOM INTO...

...our world's last great wilderness and begin a journey of great discovery. The oceans cover about two-thirds of our planet's surface, and are home to 90 per cent of all the millions of types of animals and plants that live on the Earth. All life came from the oceans, including us, yet we know very little about this incredible habitat.

Zoom inside

If you looked at a drop of ocean water through a microscope you might be shocked by what you could see – tiny animals and plants. They are called plankton, and they live in seawater. Most of them are too small to be seen with the naked eye. A microscope works by using lenses to change the way light passes through them, to make an image appear bigger.

Almost real

Ocean creatures with the ACTUAL SIZE icons are shown at their real-life size, as though they're moving across the page! Comparing the creature to a standard paperclip really helps you to understand its size.

ACTUAL SIZE

ZOOM!

THE INVISIBLE WORLD OF...

OCEAN LIFE

Camilla de la Bédoyère

QED Publishing

Editor: Amanda Askew
Designer: Andrew Crowson
Picture Researcher: Maria Joannou

First published in the UK in 2011 by
QED Publishing
A Quarto Group company
226 City Road
London EC1V 2TT

www.qed-publishing.co.uk

A catalogue record for this book is available from the British Library.

ISBN 978 1 84835 572 9

Printed in China

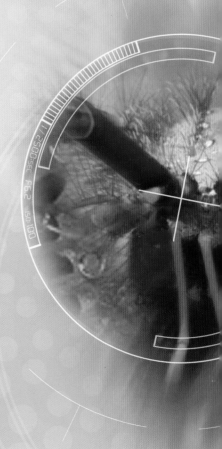

▼ Zoom into the life of a little hermit crab. These animals normally stay hidden from view, tucked away inside a borrowed shell they wear like a suit of armour.

Picture credits
Corbis Tim Pannell 4t, Carole Valkenier/All Canada Photos 9tr, Stephen Frink/Science Faction 13tr;
FLPA Hiroya Minakuchi/Minden Pictures 6–7, Ingo Arndt/Minden Pictures 7bl, Konrad Wothe/Minden Pictures 8l, Fred Bavendam/Minden Pictures 10–11, Chris Newbert/Minden Pictures 11t, Fred Bavendam/Minden Pictures 11b, Silvestris Fotoservice 17b, Chris Newbert/Minden Pictures 19t, Imagebroker 22bl, Hiroya Minakuchi/Minden Pictures 23b, Norbert Wu/Minden Pictures 27bl;
Nature Picture Library Jose B. Ruiz 9c, Mark Carwardine 14b, Jurgen Freund 18b, Georgette Douwma 21c, Jane Burton 22–23, David Shale 24t, 26b, 26–27, 27br;
Photolibrary Animals Animals/Joyce & Frank Burek 5t, Mirko Zanni 11c, Peter Arnold Images/Jonathan Bird 16l, Peter Arnold Images/Kelvin Aitken 19b, Oxford Scientific/Paulo de Oliveira 25t;
Science Photo Library Steve Gschmeissner 6b, Wim Van Egmond/Visuals Unlimited 7tr, M.I. Walker 7br, Alexander Semenov 8r, Steve Gschmeissner 9tl, Eye of Science 12t, Science Pictures Ltd 13tl, Dr. Hossler/Visuals Unlimited 13b, M.H. Sharp 14t, Alexis Rosenfeld 15b, Alexander Semenov 17tl, Kjell B.Sandved 17tr, Matthew Oldfield 18c, Peter Scoones 20t, Power and Syred 20b, Matthew Oldfield 21t, Gustav Verderber/Visuals Unlimited 22br, Wim Van Egmond/Visuals Unlimited 23t, David Wrobel/Visuals Unlimited 24b, Dr Ken MacDonald 25bl, Sinclair Stammers 27t, Power and Syred 28bl, Alexander Semenov 28br, 29tl;
Shutterstock Teguh Tirtaputra 4b, Cigdem Sean Cooper 14–15, Johan1900 15tr
Front and back cover Nature Picture Library

Words in **bold** can be found in the Glossary on page 30.

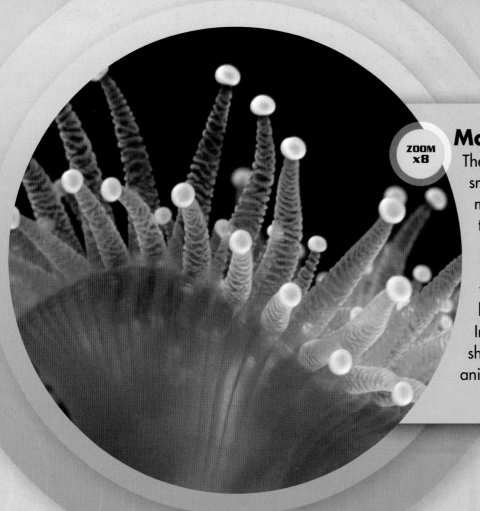

Macro photography

The art of taking pictures of small things in close-up is called macro photography. Using these, and other techniques, photographers and scientists have helped us to uncover a world we never knew existed, by giving us a fish's eye view. Images with the ZOOM icon show you how many times these animals have been magnified.

Try it

WHAT IS IT? photographs let you use your new investigative skills to guess what the sea dweller might be. Then just turn over the page to find out that IT IS…

WHAT IS IT?

ZOOM
x1500

FEEDING THE SEAS

Plankton are tiny sea creatures that act as food for the ocean's wildlife. They may be small, but they exist in billions. Plankton are eaten by fish and other sea-living creatures, and are at the bottom of the **food chain**. Most plankton live near the surface of the sea, where there is light and warmth. Antarctic krill, however, are tough little creatures.

Large eyes help krill to see in deep, dark water.

Eleven pairs of legs

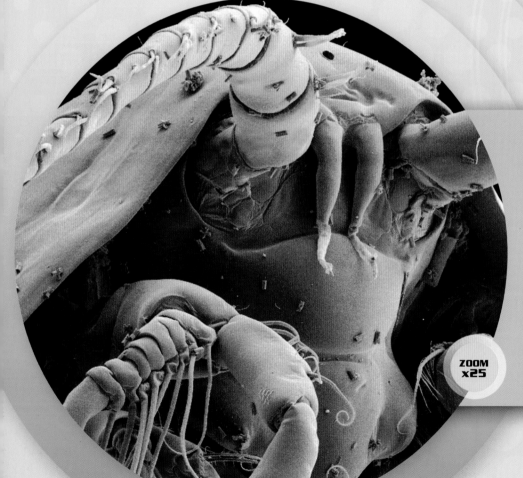

ZOOM x25

Little and large
*See a krill up close and you can make out its tough outer skin, sensory **antennae** and the special feeding limbs that filter microscopic food from the water. Most Antarctic krill are no bigger than your little finger, yet these creatures live in vast swarms and are the main food for the largest animal that has ever lived – the blue whale.*

Transparent body – light passes through

Sit or swim
*This tiny animal, called an obelia, has a strange **lifecycle**. It spends part of its life attached to the seabed, and then produces this jellyfish stage, called a medusa, and can swim. It may become food for other, larger animals.*

ZOOM x100

Krill

ZOOM x6

Tough outer skin, called a carapace

FACTOID

Krill can live in deep water, 4 kilometres below the surface, where there is no light and the water pressure would crush human bones in an instant.

It is...

a radiolarian, which is a type of plankton. Most radiolarians are too small to be seen with the naked eye. This one lived many millions of years ago and has been fossilized – turned to stone – over time.

VITAL STATISTICS

Common name	Antarctic krill
Latin name	*Euphausia superba*
Size	1–14 cm in length
Habitat	Throughout oceans
Special feature	Feed on tiny plants

MARINE MARVELS

Life began in the oceans about 3.5 billion years ago. Look closely into a rock pool at the beach, and you will begin to get an idea of the huge range of living things that still rely on the oceans for life. When you zoom in on them, you will discover strange, dramatic and incredible lives unfolding.

◄ At low tide a huge variety of living things becomes visible in rock pools, lurking between stones and in the mud.

ZOOM
x3

Star of the sea

Starfish belong to a group of animals called **echinoderms***. They usually have five arms, and their mouth is in the centre of their body, on the underside. A starfish's arms are equipped with hundreds of tiny 'tube feet' with suckers (above). They are filled with liquid, and move in waves, so the starfish can walk along the seabed.*

Caring for eggs

This tiny sea horse has just hatched from its egg. When a female sea horse lays her eggs, the male scoops them up and keeps them in a special pouch. The eggs grow here until they are ready to hatch, so they are kept safe from predators.

Catching a ride

Goose barnacles are animals that are attached to rocks and feed on plankton. A long time ago, it was thought they grew into geese, which is how they got their strange name.

ZOOM x1.5

ZOOM x30

ZOOM x30

Spiky stones

Sea urchins look like spiky stones and are a type of echinoderm. They often have venom (poison) in their spines and in their mouth, which is on their bottom! Some tropical urchins have spines that are one centimetre thick.

ACTUAL SIZE

WHat is it?

ZOOM x3

9

FLOWERY FIENDS

Jewel anemones look like beautiful underwater flowers, but they are poisonous predators. When clusters of jewel anemones live on the seafloor or on rocks, they create a carpet of brightly coloured animals. They range in colour from pink to blue and green, but their good looks hide a deadly secret.

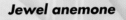
Three rings of tentacles

ZOOM
x5

Jewel anemone

ZOOM
x8

Hidden weapons
This beautiful jewel anemone has stings in its stubby tentacles. When fish or other animals swim through the tentacles, the stings are fired at the prey, injecting painful venom. Some anemones have stings that work like harpoons, catching and dragging the prey to the animal's mouth.

100 tentacles around the central cavity – the mouth

Stuck still

Anemones are sessile animals – they are attached to the rocks and rarely move. If they do move, it is very slowly. This tube anemone has a long slender body that is actually buried beneath the seabed. Some tube anemones have bodies that extend down 40 centimetres or more in the sand, mud or gravel.

ZOOM x2

FACTOID

Boxer crabs carry stinging sea anemones on their claws and wave them at any animals they want to scare!

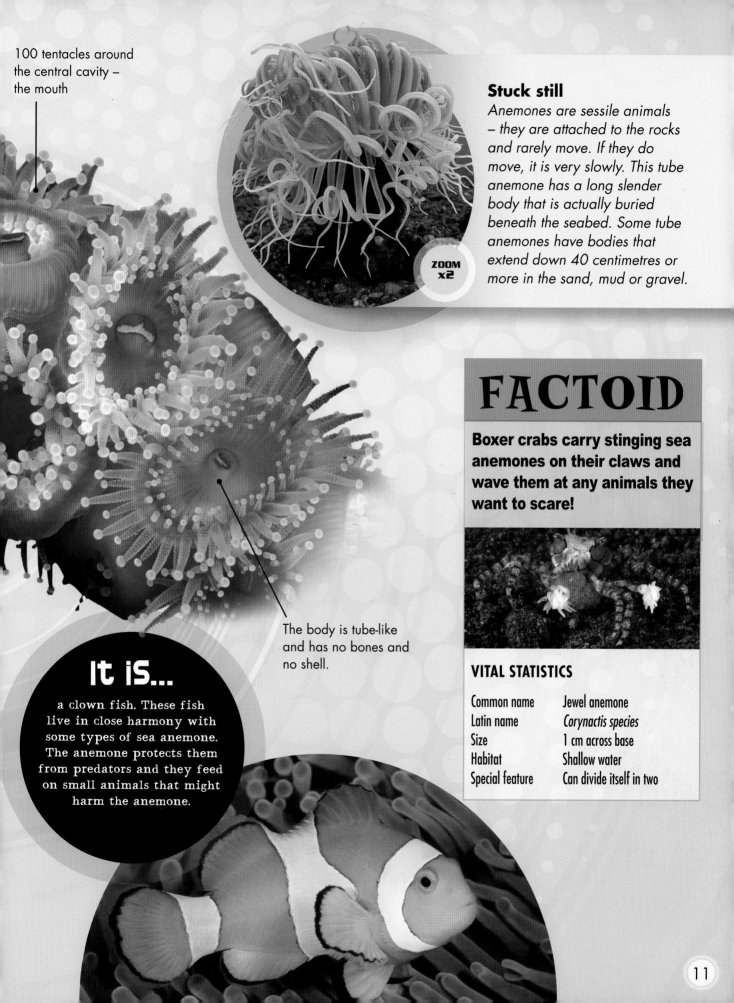

VITAL STATISTICS

Common name	Jewel anemone
Latin name	*Corynactis species*
Size	1 cm across base
Habitat	Shallow water
Special feature	Can divide itself in two

The body is tube-like and has no bones and no shell.

It is...

a clown fish. These fish live in close harmony with some types of sea anemone. The anemone protects them from predators and they feed on small animals that might harm the anemone.

FANTASTIC FISH

What is a fish? There are so many types, in so many shapes, sizes and colours, that it is hard to say exactly what makes a fish. The tiniest ocean fish are smaller than your fingernail, but the largest ones – whale sharks – grow up to 14 metres long.

ZOOM x88

◀ When a shark's skin is magnified, its extraordinary structure becomes visible. Each of these pointed scales is called a denticle and is more similar to a tooth than an ordinary fish scale.

WHAT IS IT?

Baby fish

Few fish look after their eggs or young. A brown trout female can lay 10,000 eggs at a time, in the hope that a few baby fish – called **fry** – make it to adulthood. Eggs and fry are a tasty, nutritious food for many other marine animals.

ZOOM x30

Big eyes

When divers swim up close to glasseye snappers, they get an eyeful. These night-time hunters are fish with superb vision, thanks to their huge eyes. They can grow up to 50 centimetres long and live around reefs.

Deep breathing

Seawater contains **oxygen** – the gas that fish breathe to release energy from food. Water goes into a fish's mouth and flows over its **gills**, which are located behind its head. This image of gills has been magnified to show how they have a large surface area to increase the movement of oxygen into the fish's blood. A waste gas, carbon dioxide, passes out.

ZOOM x250

13

WARNING STRIPES

When deepsea photographers want to take snaps of a lionfish, they are more likely to zoom out than zoom in! These good-looking fish don't wear their stripes for fun – they send out a clear signal that warns other animals to stay away, because those spines can hurt.

The dorsal fins carry venom, or poison.

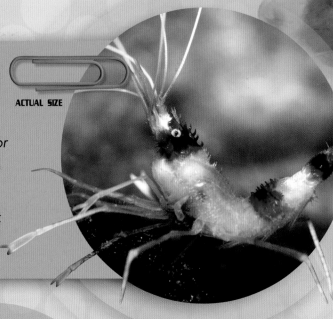

Small and spiky
*The red stripes on a banded coral shrimp may help this little **crustacean** to hide, or they may warn hungry lionfish that the shrimp has a surprise in store. Look closely at its back and you will notice a row of sharp spines.*

ACTUAL SIZE

Red-and-white stripes are a warning to predators to stay away.

It is...

a mackerel. The smooth scales on its shiny body reflect light. When a shoal of thousands of mackerel dart through the ocean they create a bright sheet of shimmering light, which confuses their predators.

Fins on the side of the body – pectoral fins – are used to trap prey against rocks or coral.

Lionfish

FACTOID

Some sharks prey on lionfish – the stinging spines have no bad effects on them.

VITAL STATISTICS

Common name	Lionfish
Latin name	*Pterois* species
Size	Up to 40 cm in length
Habitat	Coastal waters in warm places
Special feature	Venomous spines

Can you see me?
A tiny anemone shrimp is easy to miss. It has an almost transparent body, which means it can hide itself between an anemone's tentacles, or among this white coral. When you are small and defenceless, it is a good idea to use your appearance to blend in, or disappear from view – and you just might avoid being eaten by something bigger.

ZOOM x15

BONELESS DWELLERS

Animals can grow big, soft and squashy in the ocean. This is because water is thicker, or denser, than air and can support an animal's body without the need for lots of bones. Animals without bones are called **invertebrates**, and while some of them grow a tough outer skin or shell for defence, others are soft.

◀ The flamingo tongue snail has soft, patterned skin, which it wraps over its shell. It feeds on sea fans – a type of coral.

ZOOM x5

Mighty molluscs

*Sea slugs and snails belong to a group of animals called **molluscs**, and most of them live in the sea. From shelled mussels at the beach, to mighty squid in the deep ocean, molluscs have become the masters of the marine habitat. There are at least 50,000 different types, or species, of mollusc.*

WHAt iS it?

Record breaker

The longest animal ever found was an ocean worm. It was a bootlace worm and measured 55 metres in length. This ragworm grows to a mere 40 centimetres, but it looks fearsome when magnified. It has four small eyes, and two clusters of four tentacles on either side of its ugly head.

Spectacular spiral

This colourful spiral is part of a marine worm, called a Christmas tree worm. Most of its body is out of view, enclosed by a shell-like tube. This spiral is an **organ** with two jobs – it operates like gills, allowing the worm to breathe, and it captures small particles of food that might drift by.

ZOOM x8

ZOOM x2

ACTUAL SIZE

Deadly venom

Cone shells look harmless, but they fire a harpoon loaded with venom that is powerful enough to stun and kill a person. Scientists who study the venom from these marine snails hope to produce painkilling medicines.

SMALL BUT DEADLY

A blue-ringed octopus may be small, but it is deadly – with a 'hazard' warning sign to match. Zoom in close and look at those bold blue rings. They show that the octopus is feeling threatened, and is ready to attack. Its saliva, or spit, contains fast-acting venom that can kill.

Blue-ringed octopus

Yellow or light-brown skin

Toxic spike

Zoom up as close as you like to a deadly stonefish, and it may still be invisible. This camouflaged fish is one of the most venomous animals in the world. If you tread on one of 13 spines on its back you could be injected with venom that causes excruciating pain, and even death.

It is...

a giant clam. These molluscs are up to 150 centimetres in length, and do not move from the seabed. They filter small particles of food from seawater and live in the shallow waters of the Pacific Ocean.

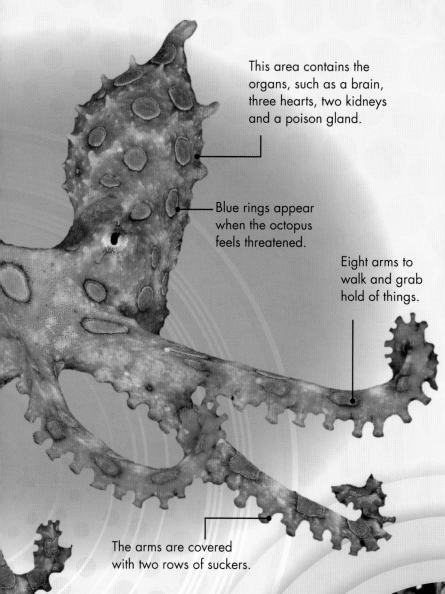

This area contains the organs, such as a brain, three hearts, two kidneys and a poison gland.

Blue rings appear when the octopus feels threatened.

Eight arms to walk and grab hold of things.

The arms are covered with two rows of suckers.

This octopus has a painless bite, but it has enough venom to paralyse ten adults.

VITAL STATISTICS

Common name	Blue-ringed octopus
Latin name	*Hapalochlaena* species
Size	10 to 20 cm in length
Habitat	Tropical areas of Pacific and Indian Oceans
Special feature	Bright-blue rings

ACTUAL SIZE

Feast or famine?

Blue-ringed octopuses feast on fish, shrimp and crabs. They bite their victim, or release poisonous saliva into the water around it. The octopus waits for the venom to take effect, then eats the prey. This mother octopus will not eat for six months while she protects her white, oval-shaped eggs. When they hatch, she will die.

COLOURFUL CORAL

Coral reefs are often called rainforests of the sea. They are special because they are home to about one quarter of all types of ocean-dwelling animals. Reefs are stony structures that are built by the tiny animals, called polyps, that live inside them.

◄ A coral polyp is closely related to a sea anemone. Like anemones, these small animals have a column-shaped body and rows of tentacles arranged around the mouth.

ZOOM x7

Super stars

Coral reefs grow over thousands of years, and create a home, or habitat, for other creatures. This small brittle star uses its five arms to walk on the seafloor, but it can quickly scuttle into crevices in a reef if it is threatened.

ZOOM x10

Hide and seek

Look closely at this coral, and try to find the soft coral crab that is hiding among its branches. Two little beady black eyes are the only clue it is present. The world's first coral reefs grew around 210 million years ago. These warm-water corals grow only in shallow, clean ocean water. The largest reef is the Great Barrier Reef, Australia. It took about 18 million years to grow and is now about 2000 kilometres long.

ACTUAL SIZE

Reefs in danger

Scientists examine coral to find out how reef habitats are changing. In recent times, large areas of reef have changed dramatically. When polyps die, the stony structures they live in turn white, and are described as 'bleached'. It is thought that pollution and **global warming** may cause even larger areas of coral to die.

ACTUAL SIZE

ACTUAL SIZE

21

HUNTING FOR A HOME

Little hermit crabs are a coral reef's clean-up brigade. They scuttle over rocky surfaces, picking up little bits of food to nibble. This helps the coral polyps to grow and stay healthy. Zoom in close to get a good look at this creature's extraordinary features.

Jointed legs for walking and swimming

Crab

FACTOID

Many crabs are scavengers and feed on dead animals. They also hunt, and may lose a claw during a battle. Thankfully, crabs can grow new legs to replace ones they lose.

VITAL STATISTICS

Common name	Scarlet reef hermit crab
Latin name	*Paguristes cadenati*
Size	4 cm (legspan)
Habitat	Coral reefs
Special feature	Lives in a borrowed shell

ZOOM x20

Time to grow
This is one of thousands of eggs laid by the horseshoe crab. The larva is growing inside, and it will take up to ten years for this animal to become an adult.

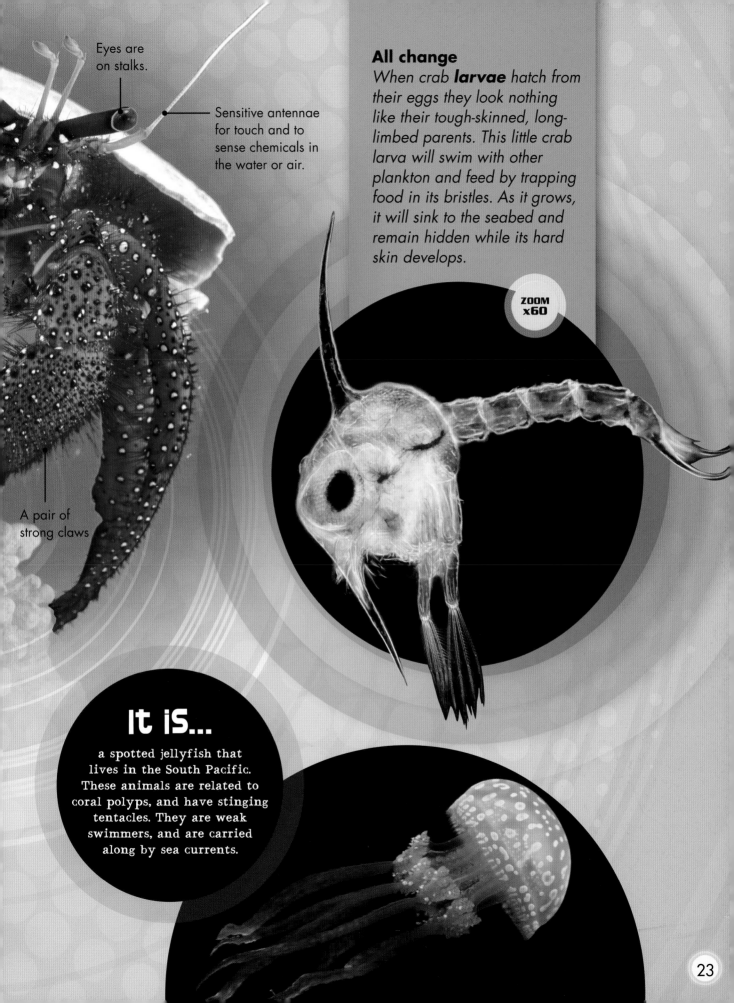

Eyes are on stalks.

Sensitive antennae for touch and to sense chemicals in the water or air.

A pair of strong claws

All change

*When crab **larvae** hatch from their eggs they look nothing like their tough-skinned, long-limbed parents. This little crab larva will swim with other plankton and feed by trapping food in its bristles. As it grows, it will sink to the seabed and remain hidden while its hard skin develops.*

ZOOM x60

It is...

a spotted jellyfish that lives in the South Pacific. These animals are related to coral polyps, and have stinging tentacles. They are weak swimmers, and are carried along by sea currents.

DEEP-SEA MONSTERS

The deeper you dive into the oceans, the darker it gets. At depths of about 200 metres, very little light can filter through, and at depths of 1000 metres, the ocean is inky-black. Zoom down into the deepest ocean zones and you'll find some of the world's most bizarre animals in extreme habitats.

ACTUAL SIZE

◀ A young glass squid is called a larva and lives near the ocean's surface with other plankton. This adult, however, survives in deep, dark water to depths of 2800 metres.

Red jelly
Ocean explorers use robots and remotely operated vehicles (ROVs) to zoom into the deepest places. They have discovered extraordinary animals, such as this small red jellyfish with its thousands of tentacles.

ZOOM
x2

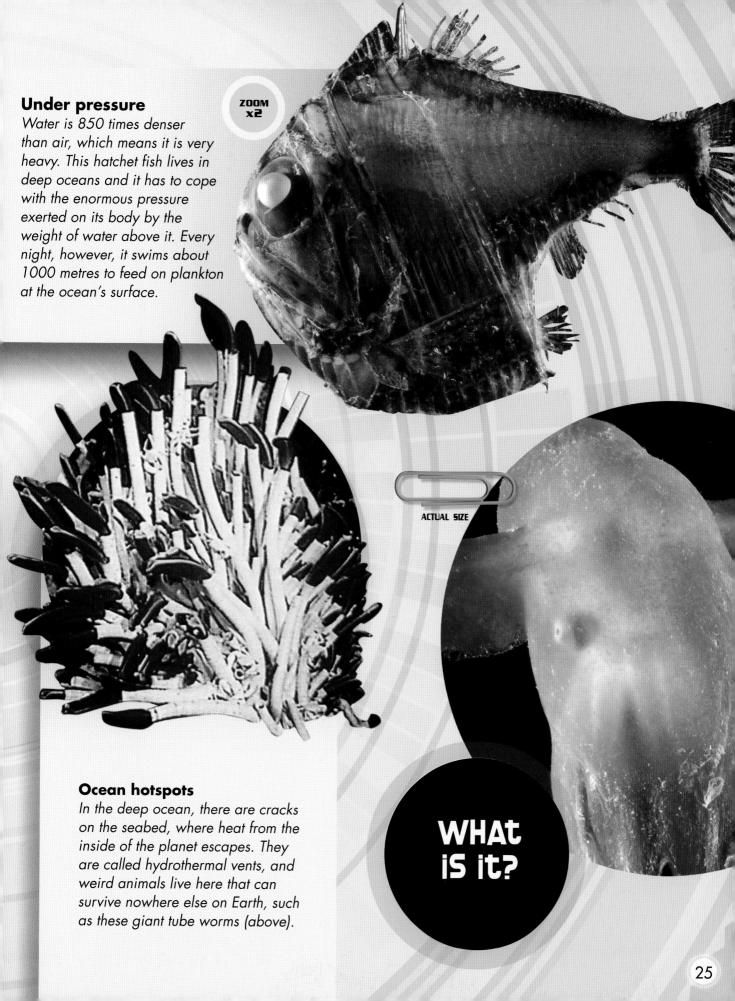

Under pressure

Water is 850 times denser than air, which means it is very heavy. This hatchet fish lives in deep oceans and it has to cope with the enormous pressure exerted on its body by the weight of water above it. Every night, however, it swims about 1000 metres to feed on plankton at the ocean's surface.

ZOOM x2

ACTUAL SIZE

Ocean hotspots

In the deep ocean, there are cracks on the seabed, where heat from the inside of the planet escapes. They are called hydrothermal vents, and weird animals live here that can survive nowhere else on Earth, such as these giant tube worms (above).

WHAT IS IT?

BRIGHT LIGHTS

The deep ocean contains many mysteries, but marine scientists are discovering new animals all of the time. One of the most incredible discoveries is the viperfish. These are powerful, fierce predators with a body that is perfectly suited to their deep-sea habitat.

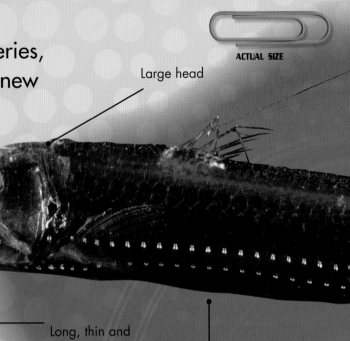

ACTUAL SIZE

Large head

Long, thin and very sharp fangs

Lines of photophores on the underside

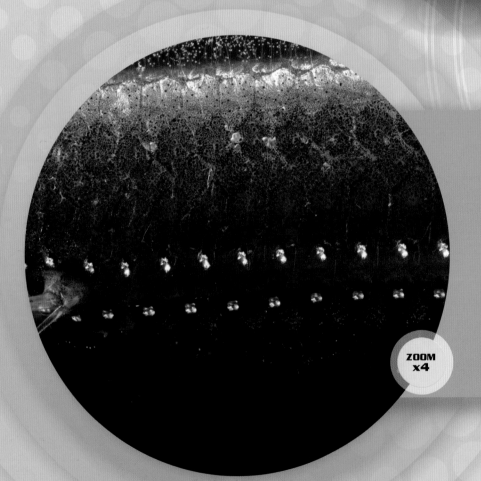

ZOOM x4

Glowing in the dark

Who needs the Sun's light when you can make your own? Some deepwater animals, including viperfish, have special places on their body, called **photophores**, *which make light. These help to confuse predators, or attract prey and mates.*

The lure contains photophores and attracts prey.

Long, thin body

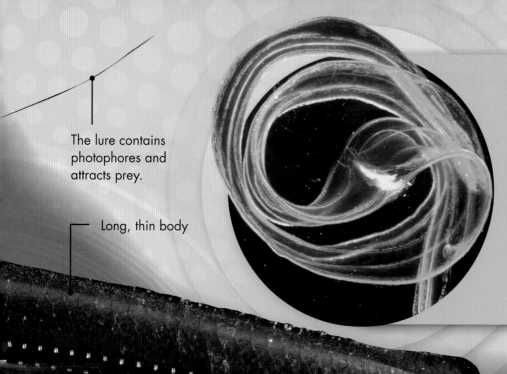

Viperfish

Glowing ribbons

This strange-looking animal is called a comb jelly. Its ribbon-like body is covered on one side with tiny hairs, called cilia. Known as Venus's girdle, this animal swims with a snake-like movement and glows greenish-gold at night.

FACTOID

A female hatchet fish is big, but her partner is tiny. He stays stuck to her body, feeding off her, and fertilizing her eggs.

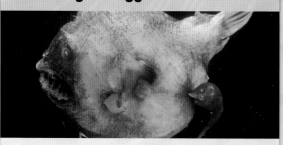

VITAL STATISTICS

Common name	Viperfish
Latin name	*Chauliodus* species
Size	Up to 30 cm in length
Habitat	At depths of 500–1000 metres
Special feature	Can make its own light

It is...

a deepwater dumbo octopus. Its tentacles are covered with small bristles called cirri. When the cirri move backwards and forwards they create water currents that drag food into the octopus's mouth.

USE YOUR EYES

Use your eyes to study these zooms that appear throughout the book. Can you recognize any of the animals just by looking at these pictures? Are there any clues, such as colour or shape, that help you work out where you've seen these images before?

1 *I am too soft to survive, so I borrow someone else's home.*

2 *I have a long journey to find food, but my body is up to the challenge.*

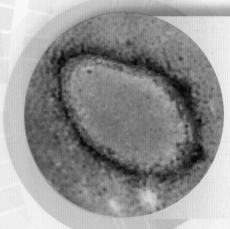

3 *I'm small but deadly, so beware my rings of blue.*

4 *I walk with my arms, how strange is that?*

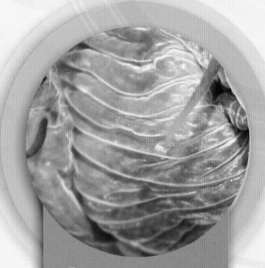

5 *My cousins can grow up to 55 metres, but I'm just ugly!*

6 Which 'fish' has both arms and feet? That's me!

7 I have a bad temper and spines to match. Divers beware!

8 Giant blue whales make a meal of me.

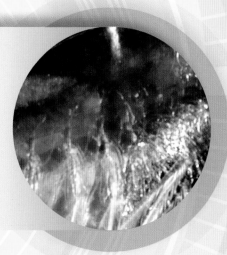

9 I am named after a large water bird, but I can't fly anywhere.

10 My cousins are slugs and snails, would you believe it?

11 If you see my fangs, you are in deep water!

GLOSSARY

Antennae Long, slender organs on an animal's head that help it to sense what is going on around it. They can usually detect touch, smell and taste.

Crustacean An animal with four or more pairs of limbs, a body that is divided into segments and a tough exoskeleton. Most crustaceans live in water.

Echinoderm A type of marine animal that is often circular in shape and has a symmetry of five. Sea urchins, starfish and brittle stars are echinoderms.

Food chain A chain of animals that depend on each other for food. Plants are normally at the bottom of a food chain; they are eaten by one animal, which is eaten by another animal, and so on.

Fry Baby fish. When they first hatch they are sometimes called larvae.

Gills Organs that are used to take oxygen out of water, and to pass the waste gas (carbon dioxide) out of the body. Fish have gills.

Global warming The warming of the Earth's atmosphere. This means the oceans are also getting hotter.

Invertebrate An animal that does not have a backbone. Molluscs, worms and insects are invertebrates.

Larva (plural: larvae) A newly hatched animal. It will eventually change and grow into an adult.

Lifecycle The way an animal begins its life, grows, reproduces and eventually dies.

Mollusc An invertebrate with a soft body that usually lives in damp places or water habitats, such as the ocean. Snails, octopuses, shellfish and squid are molluscs. Most molluscs grow shells.

Organ An area of the body, such as the brain, lung or heart, that performs a special job.

Oxygen The gas that is produced by plants, and that animals breathe to live.

Photophore An organ that produces light.

INDEX

NOTES FOR PARENTS AND TEACHERS

Photography and microscopy are two ways that the physics of light and lenses can be applied to our everyday lives. Use the Internet* to find diagrams that show how lenses bend (refract) light that goes through them. Look at diagrams that show both convex and concave lenses, to discover how the shape of the lens changes the effect. Together, you can work out which of these two types of lens is used in microscopes, telescopes and binoculars. You can also use the Internet to explore the role of lenses in the human eye, and how corrective lenses in spectacles improve eyesight.

On a sunny day you can demonstrate the focusing power of a lens. Hold a magnifying lens just above a piece of paper that is laid out in sunshine. Angle the lens until the light is focused on the paper, as a small bright dot. As it heats, the paper will smoke and burn.

It is easy to make a water lens that shows how even a simple lens can magnify images. Lay a piece of clingfilm or other transparent plastic over a piece of newspaper text. Use a syringe, or a teaspoon, to place a drop of water on the plastic. You will notice that the text beneath the water drop is magnified. Find out what happens when you make the drop bigger, or smaller.

Once you have established that water bends light, encourage the child to experiment with the way that an image can appear distorted when seen through water. Playing games with water, in troughs or at the swimming pool, provides an opportunity to see this effect.

Photography underwater has its problems. Talk about what those problems might be, and how they might be overcome. Use the Internet to investigate underwater cameras and how they work. Search ROVs (remotely operated vehicles) and deepwater submersibles, such as Alvin, to discover how scientists and explorers have uncovered some of the ocean's deep secrets.

Teach children to respect the wildlife around them. They can watch wildlife at the seaside without harming it. Encourage them to respect the animals' habitats and to disturb the environment as little as possible. Remind them that they should never play near water without an adult's supervision.

*The publishers cannot accept any liability for the content of Internet websites, including third-party websites.